Heart Well Worn

The LWAs

Stuart James

PublishAmerica

Baltimore

ISBN: 978-1-4489-6438-3
PUBLISHED BY PUBLISHAMERICA, LLLP
www.publishamerica.com
Baltimore

Printed in the United States of America

For

Kristi, my other half

And anyone who has ever had a broken heart.

Table of Contents

Author's Note & Introduction

"LWA" is an acronym for Literary Work of Art. Writing isn't simply writing to me, it's an expression of who I am and what I feel. A sketch of my heart, a portrait of my life… These words I've written express the inexpressible, my journey through love and loss, growth and acceptance. They are not simply poems; they make up the side of me you wouldn't normally see: The maturity I've gained, the severity of life, the serious side of my mind that many have never once caught a glimpse.

I assure you that each and every LWA you are about to read are 100% mine, and the emotions, musings and bewilderments contained within them are 100% true. I've split my LWAs into three parts. Part One is dedicated to falling in love, being in love, or infatuation in general. Part Two, the darker chapter of this collection, is not simply about losing love, it holds many topics such as betrayal, guilt, obsession, and most regrettably, self-mutilation. Part Three is a welcomed change of heart where I began to embrace other ideals such as friendship and family, life and freedom, among other things.

You will find that the majority of the LWAs written in 2005, are located within Part Two. As is the case for most teenagers, high school was a difficult time for me. It was a time for me to learn, grow and find myself, but I couldn't. I felt the pressure of my fellow classmates, teachers, parents, friends and siblings weighing down on me and it seemed at the time that they all expected too much of me. I became self-destructive, mostly in an emotional sense, but occasionally, unfortunately, in a physical sense as well. I'm taking this opportunity to proclaim that that was a different time and I was a different person; and I'm sorry for those who were harmed by my harming myself.

Though 2005 was easily the darkest chapter in my life, it was also a time of growth for my writing. There is a clear change from my LWAs in 2004 to those of 2005. Where in 2005 my writing describes setting and pulls metaphors prominently into the story, those written in 2004 were much more basic and juvenile. I left all LWAs written in 2004 in the exact form I found them when I stumbled upon them again in 2008. Why? Because those were the emotions I felt then, and that was how I wrote them *then*. Making changes to them now would, in my opinion, detract from their authenticity and originality.

In certain LWAs, you will find stanzas repeated. Such is the case in LWAs like "Really Gone," "Night After Night," and "When I Told You (We Were Friends Forever)." This was because I wrote them intending to record them at some point as songs. I don't consider myself a strong songwriter, but I do get inspired to write LWAs in that format occasionally.

As stated before in the Author's Note regarding LWAs and their meaning, I have difficulty being serious a lot of the time. That is, no doubt, why I turned to writing in the first place. It was a way for me to be taken seriously without compromising my sarcastic, joking attitude. However, there were times when I tried to write of topics that were on the lighter side, but they were still transcribed in an intense manner, such is the case for LWAs like "It Began With a Sneeze" and "Never Wake Me." It's OK to laugh, they were meant to be funny.

Within Part Three, there are a few LWAs that you might read and ponder why they were not placed in Part Two. These LWAs, namely "War," "SocioPsycho," and "Experience the Light," *do* seem slightly dark, but they are concluded in *me* taking control of some unnamed situation, unlike in many of the LWAs found in Part Two where giving up is seen as the only option. The control I maintained is why they were included in Part Three rather than Part Two.

Some of my LWAs have dedications, such as "Heartfire" and "29." However, chances are, over half of the LWAs included in this collection are based around one person or another. In the case of LWAs focusing on love, loss, or betrayal by one person did not receive any dedication for two reasons. One, if in the case of being in love, many times I was unable to tell that person how I felt, which is why an LWA was written. The fact remains that I don't want them to know how hard I fell, or they don't want to know I fell at all. And two, in the case of heartbreak or betrayal, dedications were not included because they don't deserve credit for hurting me.

I admit I am guilty. Many of my friends and family have never seen the serious side of me. Even now, when I'm with those I care about the most, I have a hard time being real…preferring more to crack jokes and be sarcastic. I apologize for my inability to show, more often, who I can be rather than who I think you want to see. I hope that this book of my inner-most thoughts and feelings will get you up-to-speed on all the emotion and sincerity that I haven't been able to express vocally.

With Love,
Stuart James

Part One:

Infatuation

Heartfire

Written: October 6, 2009

In this, I testify that I too hold fault
But to a friend in need I extend my hand
I don't want you to hurt and fall again
So please, take these words I speak unto you
Tailor made, inscribed with my love

If he knows not your thoughts within
An expectation is foolishly obtained
In such trial, the responsibility falls to you
Take the time in confident approach
And refer to that which you wish the most

And should you find yourself turned away
Let no eye gaze upon you next to him again
Your fragile heart...mangled once more
Don't let your heartfire slowly die, not for him
Why not carry yourself proudly out the door?

Believe in me, have faith in what I say
You don't need that boy, or his filth love

In a moment speak love to yourself
Give it a simple try and let care flit away
Believe in me, you truly are fine for now

And perhaps you find yourself right here again
Thinking you've truly fallen for another
You have to know deep down, if it is truly real?
Or have you glorified that one tiny act...
Look inside you, but don't tell me.
Tell yourself.

~Dedicated to Hannah M. Ducey~

Breath of the Victim

Written: July, October 15 and 17, 2009

They walked together, side-by-side, hand-in-hand
On that late hour on a cold winter's night
As they passed through the city's lively bustle
He pulled her close, kept her always held tight

So when that hooded, masked figure appeared
Cornered them both with a blade in hand
He fought, gave all he had to protect love
But it was soon over, his valiant last stand

And as the breath of the victim escapes his lips
Escapes one last time, he leaves behind
His legacy... he, the martyr for love, lost
Love never beheld, never again to find

They were proud, didn't believe in keeping secrets
It was known to all just who and what they were
He loved him courageously and with no bounds
With a head-spinning, heart-pounding, love blur

But there were those who did not approve
And he only had time to jump in front of the bullet
When the shot fired, here surrendered it all
And he held him in his arm's for his final minute

And as the breath of the victim escapes his lips
Escapes one last time, he leaves behind
His legacy... he, the martyr for love, lost
Love never beheld, never again to find

Desire

Written: September 15, 2008

As the smooth, gray smoke
Curls around my head,
Creating intimate paintings
of unnatural toxicity,
I become consumed in the stillness.
Consumed by the thoughts of unlife.
Yearning for one, simple desire
The desire to be bitten.
Unaware of my inward insanity,
Life stays on track
Around me, continues.
Casually, boringly, tediously, life.
I stay. Lost in shadow.
Hidden. Masked behind a smile.
Lying to the face of temptation.
Claiming it doesn't leave me writhing.
But when the answer to life
Is to end it all,
Where is the chilling touch
I long to reach for me?
The deadly desire pleasantly infuriates

Bite me, free me, take me
Away from sick human existence.
Curious... venomous... you'll find me.
Heart pure. Black.
Against all possibility,
The realm of undead fantasy
Calls to me, screams to me.
Inching closer to the edge
Dusken comfort and ashen faces
Inviting the pain in transformation
Welcoming gladly, the change will fulfill.
Bite. Bleed. And fall into love.
While the poison spreads,
So shall the smile across your alabaster face.
Because you love me. And I, you.
Now, forever... eternally,
Love. In blissful, beautiful darkness.

Fall for a Boy

Written: August 5, 2009

I know I shouldn't but I do;
Who wouldn't fall for a boy like you?
There isn't a sight I'd love more...
Then to find you standing at my door.
Burning to say these words at last...
But is it possible to abandon your past?
Unsurprised... to find myself disabled.
Was I not told that true love was fabled?
Shall I forever always bear this curse?
Will it continue, remain to get worse?
Never can I bring myself to get as close as I want to be
To those who are becoming the most important ones to me.
But if this could be love, I don't want to hide...
I want you, more than anyone, to know what's inside.

The Story of You Saying Yes

Written: (2005/2006?)

As you sit alone, completely unaware
The urge to tell you erupts in the air
My heart sends the message to my brain
While my insides twist uncontrollably with the strain
Heart pounding faster, my feet begin to move
Unaware of why, for my conscience wouldn't approve
My eyes transfixed on you, you gaze elsewhere
Not sure what to say, "Can we talk over there?"
As our eyes lock together, I'm almost lost
Your gaze suddenly solemn, cold as frost
I turn to walk away, and you follow after
Deep down, I remember your music of laughter
Slowing my pace, my heart leaps to my throat
Turning to you, I ignore memories of words that I wrote
Unable to speak, but I try my best
Hoping to myself that my words you won't detest
"Here is the thing..." I begin to explain
Infatuation is not something I feign
It's how you've lured me in, I can't get away
And if you want to hit me, that's completely OK
Finally, that no matter what you choose to do

I will always love and care for the magic that is you
Your eyes are filled with complete, utter shock
But your face is still solid as rock
You raise you hand and, expecting the worst,
I brace myself... ready for hurt
But a surprise on my cheek; warm, soft and light
I open my eyes to you smiling bright
Suddenly I realize, it's your hand on my face
I was not expecting a tender embrace
Terribly confused, my heart still soars
I reach with my hand and place it on yours
Smiling again, you lean towards me
Gently and quietly, you whisper free
All I have been most dying to hear
The words, "I love you" drift in my ear
Now you tell me all that I've done
The things that you love, and that I had won
Your heart is mine you tell me at last
Never again will I think of the past
Shimmering tears shine in my eyes
I lean into your chest and our arms arise
I hold you tightly in this unbelievable hug
Knowing I probably shouldn't feel so smug
My tears will fall, but I still smile
Your warm embrace comforting all the while
Slowly I pull away from your chest
And place my hand on your face to caress
Your deep, brown eyes are glimmering now
With tears you shed, but I didn't know how
I move away slightly, place my hands on your arms
You aren't aware of your magnetic charm
You lean again and this time I know

What's going to happen, nervous though
Your soft, warm lips brush light against mine
And the chills I'd expected race down my spine
Our first kiss, so sincere and sweet
But I could faint from the inner heat
As our lips part, I place my hands on your neck
Framing your head in a way you'd expect
I pull you in close and won't loosen my hold
Because I finally have you and I'll never let go.

Can't Make Me Not

Written: September 9, 2009

I try hard to smile all through the day
Knowing you might never look at me that way

Nevertheless, I hold my head up high
I'd rather let my dreams reach the sky

Together, I lose myself in your brilliant smile
When you speak, intently I listen all the while

You've always got such a sparkle in your eye
And when we hug I wonder if I've died

I keep a smooth, brave face most of the time
'Cause I don't want you to leave me behind

I take care to keepsake our memories
Locked away in my heart with no extra keys

Even though I know it may not happen
I strut through the fear, fingers snappin'

'Cause it's becoming ever-easier to see
That even closer friends we'll soon be

And even if we don't reach that further mark
Because you may not ever feel that spark,

There's still nothing that I can do
I just can't make me not love you

Night After Night

Written: Summer 2009

Babe, there was a reason I waited so long
To let you know what it was I felt
At the time I was sure you were wrong
Now looking back I'm, oh, so ashamed

All that I did and all that I said
Purely instinctive... and I didn't think
Now night after night, there's you in my dreams
And the truth's tearing through, right at the seams

I don't want to admit it but I know now it's true
Everything you say, but more what you do
Pulls me in tight and I'm stuck like glue
I'm totally and completely not over you

I've done it now... gave in to this love game
But now I have to know if you feel the same
I know there's no chance I'll survive the wait
But I'll have to endure that shame I hate

Won't settle for anything less than honesty
So tell me true, do you ever miss me?
Can you see me holding you in my arms?
The way I saw me, lost in your charm?

I don't want to admit it but I know now it's true
Everything you say, but more what you do
Pulls me in to tight and I'm stuck like glue
I'm totally and completely not over you

Unreal Hero

Written: September 25, 2008

I found you through the gift of word writ
Now, I write to keep you with me always
I want nothing more than for you to reach out
Touch the skin on my cheek with your cold hand
I long to kiss your lips and inhale your sweet breath
Continue to feel you within every essence of my being
I can be with you through perpetual, literary affection
Never have my words flowed so smoothly, effortlessly
I see in your golden eyes, the reflection of myself, meek
But to write the truth uninhibited makes me valiant
I know what is real, and you are not. I'm not insane
Yet the temptation to enhance this passion consumes me
I will stay in this devastatingly hopeless love
Lost, always, in the words you will never speak

A Dream I Found

Written: October 17, 2009

In a dream I found, it's you I see
Just across that room smiling back at me
We run away, far from those who don't matter
Between dusty pages, beyond all the chatter
I fight euphoria, attempt to be just here
Where in your eyes I see no hint of fear
I don't believe it's happened this way
This, that you and I have become today
Scenes of old may still go reeling by
I won't give in, won't release that cry
Because here and now you're all mine
When I find myself in your arms divine
Joy alight, can't keep my feet on the ground
Let's show the world the love we've found
They may judge, yes, they will scorn
But thanks to you, my heart is reborn
That smile proves your admiration pure
And I'll love you forever, that's for sure

Thunderhead

Written: April 30, 2009

Saw you once or twice before
And today you can't take it
You know you wanna be with me

It may be a raging storm all around
But I've only ever been ready
So let's take the one blind leap

I won't wait for this one second more
Make it happen, take a chance
Throw myself into the thunderhead

Take my hand, share this moment with me
Run a finger through my hair and gaze
Look deep into my eyes, that's where my love lies

And I can't wait to pass the time
Spend my day with someone like you
Because you, oh you, you're my everything

Consumption

Written: 2004

I can't think
My heart aches
Crazed obsessions
Consume my mind

Far beyond what
I've felt before
My emotions rage
Like a World War

Shrieking aloud
Crying at night
Fighting to live
Somehow surviving

Feelings abruptly
Take me away
Forever I'll feel
Forever this way

A Breathtaking Wait

Written: 2004

I've told her all I know
She says she's so confused
And doesn't know what to do
Well that makes two of us

It's like torture to think of him
And how he treats her
How could he do that?
And why?

It's all a crazy roller coaster
That is how it seems
I think of her
And my heart leaps

I know it's crazy
Being this young
And feeling the way I do:
It's love, I'm sure

No one understands
Not even her
How much I care
About her

She's so wonderful in every way
Her hair, her eyes, her face
So beautiful
All of her

Her voice is an amazing melody
So sweet and soft
Her smile fills me with indescribable joy
So intoxicating

I've never felt this way before
I feel lost right down to my core
I'm crazy for her
And she knows

But it's her choice
Him or me
Hearts at stake
A breathtaking wait.

Always. Forever. You.

Written: Winter 2005

Closing my eyes to picture your face
A smile so wide, eyes so pure
I keep my eyes closed tightly
To keep this image with me now
Watching you be my marvelous angel
Never ceasing to surpass expectations
Believing you are dying to break out
Escape your shell, revive your soul
When you emerge, I feel you should know
I'll be expecting your glowing face
That's what love is...
Waiting for it to be returned
And since you're the one I love
I shall wait for the reciprocation.
Always. Forever. You.

Save Me Love Tonight

Written: 2004

Stranded out here
Scared and alone
Someone will find me
They will, I know

No one would leave me
Out here on my own
Deep in this forest
Lost sorrows will grow

They'll grow so large
Overcoming all my strength
I'll have to hold on
All on my own, this night

Can I do it? Can I make it?
Tell myself, "Yes, yes I will."
I have a power far too strong
Love, love will guide me

It has in the past…
And so it will now…
Save me love tonight

Won't You (Fall for Me)

Written: Winter 2005

I've dealt with plenty of emotion before
None quite compare with this specific swell
You're not the type I normally fall for
Still, I am in that painful love again
I see you, I blush. I think of you, I cry inside.
This dam in my eyes, holding in my tears
Won't it crumble away? Let all inhibitions go
I yearn to fall into your arms...or you into mine
Something...anything...As I gaze into your eyes
Can I be the one to trace your young heart?
Mine is completely swollen. This has to be it
I'm tired of falling for no one to catch me
Praying you'll love me, infatuated. I'll love you
So tell me, please, won't you be the one to fall for me?

Not Thinking of You

Written: September 2008

You are a distorted craze
I've never before stumbled upon

You are my affection

No matter how much I focus
On not thinking of you...

You are my addiction

The vision of intimacy that
Will never come true

You are my obsession

You And All You Do

Written: September 19, 2009

Had a busy day today but couldn't get you off my mind
It's you and all you do, and it drives me crazy
That it's this impossible to find my way to you
You can't help where you are, it's no more your fault than mine
And we may not know each other all that well yet
But more often than not, I find myself yearning
I can't help but wonder from time to time again
Am I wasting my time? What do you see in your future?
Can you tell me...Is it me you're holding out for?
I feel I should make you aware of one small fact
You could have so much more, so much better than me
There could be many who would die to be with you
And most would rather die than be with me
I know there is no one else, not a single one
That's been gone way away from me this long
And yet I find myself still undeniably crazed
You're the only one who has never once ignored my desires
When every time before I've been welcomed into rejection
I find acceptance in you and your forgiving heart
I'm ready to be taken seriously and I know you do
For that reason, I only want to be with you

Part Two:
Disappointment

Really Gone

Written: August 2008

On the outside, painted on my face
A ray of sunshine, bright and warm
But I am lost in an imaginary place
A field of dreams where love rains down
Like manna from heaven
No pain, no desperation
Smiles all around

Why does every broken love song
Remind me of myself?
Time has passed and lives have changed
Oh no... Is love really gone?

On the inside written in my heart
Deceiving lies that love is just a myth
But I'll burn that book and all its lies within
Ignite it in the truth

Life's not got me down
I'm just in a rut

Musings of love have left me
Stranded in this slump

Why does every broken love song
Remind me of myself?
Time has passed and lives have changed
Oh no... Is love really gone?

Ever Anywhere

Written: August 27, 2009

It exists everyday, surfacing always the same way;
When a thought occurs and keeps you stirring,
The mind locks down from constant pressure;
And hair upon the neck begins to stand on end
While the ever-swelling heart suffocates the lungs.
As the body is taken over with uncompromisable emotion,
The logic of conscience is drowned out far too rapidly.
That everlasting tug on everywhere inward
Keeps the mind lingering on that one thought:
You believe in your soul there might just be something.
But take heed, he will never know that something.
And now something's nothing. So it won't go. Ever anywhere.
At some point, you'll be forced to throw it all away.
Deep down you know that what you want you'll never get;
So though you may want with all your heart to reach out,
You will have to give it up in one simple surrender.
Have no fear, it can be one glorious last stand against such
twisted emotion.
No doubt you shan't be the last to admit defeat in the battle
of love.

Infected Dreamland (I'll See You Soon)

Written: 2005, September 26, 2008

I awake.
Every night from nightmares of you.
Then, I dream for them to become the real.
Pain sears my body as I lie here
Wishing I won't dream of you again
What I wouldn't give to sleep sound
Yet dream again of you and your face
If only to combine my two only hopes
My desire is, as always, my despair
Somehow, in Dreamland, is where you find me
This is where you choose to hurt me
The pain you create hunts. Craves. Destroys.
It feeds on those few hopeful, happy memories
The ones brave enough to dare show their faces
This infection spreads fast as it devours
Because every time that spark emerges...
...Shines just a little bit bright...
It's always been ignited by a false belief
That love might have actually found me...
...whether in Dreamland or the World
Nay, I am no believer in love

You have made damn sure of it
Yet I am deceived again as the sun sinks down
I look forward to the nightly hour
When I shall see your face once more
I pray for the haunting memory
Of you and what you do to me
I can only count on you loving me there
Nowhere else...only in my infected Dreamland
You'll love me there, and I'll love you always
Goodnight, daylight. Welcome, moonlight.
I'll see you soon...

The Raven's Momentary Shelter

Written: 2005, September 19, 2009

The Raven calls out and I listen intently
I feel it is trying to say what I need to hear
This treacherous storm roars and rages around me
My blurred vision impairs my reason
Closing my eyes I bring myself to resist
I fight the urge to embrace the once-trusted darkness
I turn my mind over to better understand the Raven
Swirling winds and raging water try ferociously to drown me
It is here I find myself aware of the Raven's mission
A rescue. The Raven is trying to save me
Desperately I cling to its words, for they shelter me
Rescue me, Raven, from this never-ending storm
The barren heart within me cries out in bloodstained agony
Dying...suffocation from the lack of its key nutrient: Love
With the words of the Raven, I am only minimally safe
For the walls are caving in on me now
There's no match for the tumultuous rage beating down upon them
Fleeing from the shelter as it collapses, I can outrun
But I won't be ahead forever, this storm always finds me
I run with tears streaking down my cold face
Through the empty streets of unquestionable familiarity

I've been here many times before, it's always the same
I pray the storm shan't regain its fury and
Pull me back inside its murderous grip
The only weapon I have must be replenished in time...
...But time is slipping away...
Where is the Raven now?

Where Does My Heart Turn

Written: Early Spring 2009; Rewritten: June 25, 2009

There was a time
When I would give anything
Just to hold you in my arms

There was a time
When you would be there
Always there for me

Things are different now
When our lives flashed by
I can't hold on to what we had

This time I think it's really over
I wasn't ready to say goodbye
Wasn't ready to let you go

This time I think it's for real
Though I'll never stop dreaming
Can't keep myself from love

I can't tell who I am now
And what should come next
Where does my heart turn?

Was it my own damn fault?
Was it what you did to me?
Can't figure out what should change

One foot over the edge
Not gonna take that last step
But what is holding me here?

So Now I Lay Unmoving

Written: 2005

Once again, I find myself emotionless
Unable to pinpoint these distortions
I lay among the ashes of my previous lies
Silently drowning in the sin I commit
Immobile and weak, gasping for breath
Having grown accustomed to consumption
So I wait for the wave to break, to be free
Freedom will be short-lived, I will be here again
But I can't resist hoping for a momentary lapse
False happiness that creates such intricate lies
Releasing my acidic tears to burn my flesh away
My countenance growing weak, deceiving me
Misled. Believing that these earthly untruths
Are beautiful roses, waiting to be admired
Yet the disguise is incomplete, thorns visible
Naive and afraid, I reach with hope despite
And the pain has been inflicted, a job well done
So now, I lay, unmoving and untrusting
As I recall a life that never was and never will
Belief that fulfilled was just another deception

Since these lies are absolutely inescapable
I'll go on loving, go on lying, go on dying
Slowly and painfully...until death settles me

Weather Experience

Written: October 4, 2009

A synthetic melody takes me home
But it isn't the home I choose to recall
As fear, anger & resentment succeed in mutiny
I feel a fire ignite, spark within my veins
It rages. It spreads. It destroys.
All a forgotten, suppressed memory of anguish
These emotions build, they grow and mutate
And when a gust of wind changes my soul's direction
I feel lost in such is this, a weather experience
Because my brilliant sun-soaked day has darkened
Suddenly, I am swept up in a stormy battlefield
The cannon of thunder, the gun-shot of lightening
They leave me terrified... as I am defenseless
Now the torrential downpour attempts to drown me
And as the fire within continues to rage,
I am left to drown, cowering in regret.

Asunder

Written: August 6, 2009

The moon is beautiful tonight
You leave myself alone to be
As certain lyrics bring you here
Humidified discomfort begins to weigh
Disheartened by what that mirror sees

A light shifts from green to red
To pass a thick white finish line
When lightening abrupt collides aside
Screams from no one shatter the air
In an instant my life falls asunder

Walk in sadness, ride in danger
Skip to the chapter at the end
The one in which I give my life to you
For I am no longer driven to live it
I join the moon and stars in a pristine sky

Thank You for the Secret

Written: 2005

Now that you've done it
Now that you've crushed me
All that I am, broken
All that I felt, ignored
I have but one thing left
I have but this to say
Thank you for the secret
Thank you for keeping it
It was hard to man up
It was hard to face you
But I can survive
But I can revive
It was the world I feared
It was what they would say
Had they found me out
Had they heard of this
You know what boy
You know what sucks
If you had not second guessed
If you had chanced a yes
I would have been proud

I would have shouted it loud
All I wanted was you
All I wanted was love
I could've risked my life
I could've put it on the line
Because I cared about you
Because I always will
You're the boy so vulnerable
You're the boy I'm crazy for
Only time will show you now
Only time will tell you how

Phantom's Tears

Written: 2004

The lightweight figure moves soundly across the floor.
Creeping silently up to the third door.
It peers into this room, once beaming with light
To remember the life once lived before, was quite a sight
The vivid emotions of rage and hurt caused the light to flicker
Somehow he felt the pain of another, one who was sicker.
He took the burden upon himself, and set the other free.
Now to still the beating of an empty heart, unable to see.
Could life have found a way, a way through?
Simply complicated are the only words true.
Surging emotions of pain and sorrow, of hate and fears
Have caused the downpour of the phantom's tears...

Hidden In Icy Winter

Written: 2005

Desperation uncomprehendable
Unable to keep still, mind racing
Images of past, flash before my eyes
Forever haunting me presently
Awake. Asleep. They won't let me be
In this desolate winter, the fire burns me still
Solitude as a companion, sorrow as my friend
I sit in lonely silence as I ponder what has past
Ears ringing loudly, feelings of betrayed emotion
Stir somewhere inside this cold, dead soul
Darkness once light, grief once joy
My heart once alive, beating swiftly and willingly
Beats now forced, and full of nothing but regret
Somewhere, somehow, something keeps me alive
Maybe I'll find it, perhaps I already know
To me, this bleak, dark winter holds no answers
Nothing but untruth and chilling fear
Fear of unwelcomed love and hate
Fear of returning passion and despair
For now, I'll stay hidden in this icy world

Pain reflected in the mirror of my past
And my shadowy future revealed grim

Come Help Me, Come Near

Written: 2004

Screaming so loudly
Someone should hear
Someone come help me
Someone come near

Darkness steps in
Drowning my vision
Denying my sight like
Death by head-on collision

Intricate whispers
Invalidate my mind
Into this sea of dark
Inward they'll find

Screaming so loudly
Someone should hear
Someone come help me
Someone come near

What Could Be Wonderland

Written: 2005

Here I sit, buried
The snowcaps of this depression
Weighing down on my lungs
Harder to breathe in frigid air
Again I try to hide
The snow falls heavier
Stuck in this emotional blizzard
Becoming one with the ice
Frozen, solid, dead.
But why stay in this winter?
When the love, unreturned, consumes
The care for someone so undeserving
Trampled into this snowy grave
Icy knives pierce my cold skin
Chilling my ever-cold blood all the more
A toxic frozen poison in the cold
Polluting what could be wonderland
So cool me, chill me, freeze me, kill me
Because the numbness has taken over
And I will not feel it, now or ever

Cleanse this pure-white painting
By removing me from it forever

63

The Latter, Desperation

Written: September 25, 2008

Once settled in repetitive habit
Comforting. Unaffected. Until the rain falls
Salty in the open wound
Burning all ease away...ashes left behind.
Stirring in this unease. Fueling flames.
Anxiety flows unwillingly steady
Coursing through in overwhelming intensity
Too prominent to ignore
Too threatening to acknowledge
The power, lost. The latter, desperation.
Newly awakened, searching through the blinding eclipse
Shade the eyes. Cover with lies.
Just say, "It's OK. It'll all be over soon."
In rejection, neglection, self-destruction will arise
Suddenly, defensively, compromises enhance guilt
Left with nothing. A shadow of former familiarity
Haunting subconsciousness, daily and nightly
Drenched in cold sweat uncomfort
From the dream you had, you awake
Into the nightmare you live, you return

Martyr

Written: (2004/2005?)

It doesn't seem fair
To be punished for love
When the care I have inside
Is not returned, but
That can be endured
But to be a martyr
It just doesn't seem right
A fate worse than death
To die without love
To be made unfathomable
When you died FOR it

Take One, Pass It On

Written: October 7-9, 2009

Summer days progressed, and I began to detest
I'd perfected that plan to live life carefree
Even if only for those few short months
It was simple enough, I saw it to be
But as it wore on, it in turn wore me down
I started to fret, and with myself I fought
As you dangled me crudely over the shark tank
It was clear to us all: You liked me, or so we thought
I felt I could trust you, so I asked for your help
It was my heart I humbly requested you hold
Missing pieces already, from those that had past
But I believed in your soul, saw it shimmering gold
Now I find myself a fool, you proved a spineless oaf
Did you not realize this was no worthless pawn?
Apparently not, since you chipped off another piece
But I suppose that's fine. Take one, pass it on.

Give it away, since it's clear you don't care
I loved you then, probably shouldn't, it's true
But when I needed you most, you weren't fucking there
So leave me be, I don't want to see your face

I've lived this before, don't get me wrong
But you toyed with my mind and dragged this on
I hate that I see you when I hear that love song
I swing a bat to that window and the picture it shows
You should probably know that this is your fault
Because of what you've done, I've sent love away
My heart won't be found, secured in the vault
And I shall make everyone believe, I won't love again
I'll still send you the invitation, reluctantly
You're attending the funeral. The one for this love
Pick up your program and read of how you destroyed me
Yeah, I suppose that's fine. Take one, pass it on.

REFLECTION/prediction

Written: 2006

Defining moments unleash the storehouse of pain...
Screams of heartache...gasps in terror...
Shall destroy the safe place we have constructed...
And the reflection...lost hope will laugh in our faces...
Shrieking in ecstasy at the downfall...of all we lost...
Excerpts of past happiness flash before our blind eyes...
Reminding us that sadness has set in...
Less defined in a season of blood lust...
Where bodies lose control and all are slain...
The deception of tempting demons will lead us...
To the doorway of sin and death...we will accept...
And therefore...We Lose.

Lies Lies Lies

Written: 2006

Piercing my back
Your ruthless selfishness
Finding the truth
In compromising ways
Destroy my faith
Honesty sucked away
Trouble with communication?
A sacrificial lamb
The one to inform of you
Deception dripping out easy
Cruelly smiling
Secretly destroying
Promises broken
All that was true
Now an evil embrace
Slyly lying
Smirking in fluorescence
Regret? Legacy?
No, now easily forgettable
I won't recall
And don't remember me

If It Wasn't For Me (I'm Sorry for Loving You)

Written: Fall 2005

You said yes.
What could have possibly convinced your conscience?
Do you not see? I am but a black hole for you
Not your salvation...never the redeemer in love
Now you can't escape me. Trapping you, hurting you.
But you only want to fix me...How noble. How fatal.
Apparently, that thought unable to alter.
The infection within, has spread further than I imagined
A deadly poison: Me. This, I will forever be
No kiss, no touch, no love, no more.
Unable to risk contact in such a condition
Perpetually, forever... a danger to your sanity
If heartbreaker is the label you choose to stick
I'm breaking yours...you have to escape.
Get out soon. Leave this place, leave me.
Before you become trapped forever as I
Regretful, for memories. Apologetic, for time lost
All this time you've wasted with me
If it wasn't for this... If it wasn't for me

The simplicity of your life could have remained
But it was a mistake, your mistake. You said yes.
You should have rejected this twisted heart
Because now I must deny yours, deny you.
I'm sorry you love me...I'm sorry I love you
But please, before I drown you with me
Leave me. Escape me. Save yourself.
And please don't look back, never back on us.

Ruined

Written: November 2005

As I think of you and the words you chose,
I cry my now bloodstained tears.
They've fallen at last as I knew they would.
This is the moment I expected,
Not so soon, but I did what I was needed.
And I'm gonna keep on feeling for you.
A longing that remains as long as do I,
Though that road may soon be a dead end.
I'm tired of the post-confessional denial.
This fire within used to burn for you.
Now it just burns me.
But I still want you. You still reject me.
You will always be in my heart.
My burned, scalded heart.
After all, it wouldn't be burned if not for you.
I want you, with all that's left of my ruined heart.

The Face of the Deceiver

Written: 2006

When I look into the face of the deceiver that corrupted my soul,
I scream inward loudly enough to send my insides into a
revolted frenzy
The mark of a deceiver is clear, and easy to recognize
Repeatedly smirking at the pain found in someone else's eyes
Yet suddenly aghast at any snide comment sent their way
A truly selfish nature flows through their very bloodstream
It becomes revealed in the words they attempt to make you believe
The mouth is covered in gruesome, unseen lies.
Their eyes flicker with hints of greed,
yet shine with intimate, luring beauty
So take heed, you unexpectant...
Do not let yourself become caught
Flee before you find yourself trapped by the tempting deceiver
Stay safe and beware those who try to draw you in
With the inhuman things they do and say.

Inevitable

Written: 2005

In irony, I find an inability within myself
Focusing on anything has become unclear
As the chill of the ice runs through my veins
I remember those dreams of previous attempts, failures
All consumed me, some more than others, one remaining
Untouched since the end of a year of obsession
I vividly depict the memory of that beautiful face
And, in turn, destroy my inner being
That will pass. What shall never be done...is done
I have to move and get past the memories
Fatal, destructive thoughts that clouded my vision
Dreams of kisses in the rain...
The proclamation of undying love...
And the belief that one might change for me...
All will be slain and thrown out of my bruised heart
The consumption, obsession and eventual desolation are inevitable
But I'm sure I'll welcome them nevertheless

A Little Bit of Poison

Written: September 9, 2009

Mutilation. Destruction.
An invasive, pervasive lust.
As deathly love approaches
Escape becomes the only exit
Curl around my head and hands
Surround me. Consume me.
Spent too much time in my head
Now it's clogged, almost dead.
Take me away. Keep me company
Glide across the heavy air
When love becomes forever pain
Fear is now the deadly virus
So many symptoms. Driven insane.
I'll escape to my asylum...
It's just a little bit of poison
But it calms me down...always

You Can't

Written: 2005

The thought of you trying to "love" me
Encourages me to hate the mere thought of you
If the love you proclaimed was real
You'd accept me for the me that I am
The "love" you cling to so dear
Is an obsession, enforced regulation
Stop this futile attempt at change
The more you try to pull me in
Harder, I will force myself away
My mind has been set, alarm armed
But time is a thing of the past
All but completely run out
This game we've been playing...
You don't know the rules
Because I said I was finished, I won
You will never accept the inevitable
And it's time to end it
The end drawing nearer on the horizon
I hope it will be painful...for you
The cruelty is second nature to ME
Bring on the bloodshed, the heartache

There is nothing. I am nothing.
You can't save me...you can't change me
So leave me now...
And spend the remaining days
Remembering the better memories
If you can.

Prayer for Answers

Written: October 4, 2008

They're still here, Lord
Building up... itching to take control
They won't leave. They're inside of me
Tearing my body apart
Pieces. Pieces. That's all that's left
I can't stop the tears
Lord, where are my answers?
I'm so lost. So confused.
Nothing seems right now
I can't tell where my head is
I can't tell where my heart is
I can't tell where my life is
I'm so desperate for anything
Open the door for me please
I'm begging now for these things I've never said
I just can't say. All I'm asking for is answers
I'm willing to turn to You
Anything that will satisfy my craving
I just need to know what's happening
And please, Lord, make the dreams stop

I won't wake myself anymore
The tears are truly burning now
I'm ready to listen.

A Carefully Assassinated Heart

Written: 2005

I scream my blood-curling scream in the dead of night
Unable to comprehend the foreboding shapes surrounding me
Those blood-thirsty beings that ferociously tear at my heart
My frail heart. Unable to endure much more
Stitched together hundreds of times before
Torn apart again by those who laugh ruthlessly at my humiliation
I cower in the dark corner of life. The only place my heart can hide
In the arms of solemn loneliness,
so tired of being torn down and ripped apart
Mortal. I can only withstand so much. Shaking violently inside
My trembling soul fears a deceptive, poisonous love
It could easily sneak its way into my shy, trusting heart
Plant the virus and watch it spread...taking over my nerves
Slowly, agony consuming. And the traitor laughs at my
weakness, sickness
Yet sadly, I shall not perish...no.
I shall live on infecting all those closest to the person I used to be.

Piece Me

Written: October 4, 2008

The clock keeps inching time forward
If only to stop for a moment
A timeless moment in the stillness
Channel the confusion into focus
Suffer in the passing seconds
Yearning. Searching the blackness
Gasping for answers in a gas chamber of doubt
Images burned into this rebellious mind
Clean my slate. Escape into reality
Driven to be lost, this time in truth
Believing again, not sure why
Yet the urge in recklessness increases
Domination by self-destruction
Desperately searching for an escape
Where are the words I long for?
No longer flowing with ease as before...
What is happening in my head?
Shrieking louder and louder in silence
Tears stream down in painful invisibility
Shrouded in a fog of answerless mystery
Where is the rain? Wash it all away...

Cleanse the soul. Fulfill the need.
Piece me together...I'm ripped apart
Shine on me. Enlighten.
Searching. Asking. Searching. Asking.
The answers aren't in these tears...
So stop falling.

Bitter Contemplation

Written: 2005

time is flying by now
life is unraveling brokenly
secrets bleeding out
trusted friends lying again
tired of feeling used.
exhausted. inferior.
lies are raging rapidly
life is just another wasteland
wasted. devastation. again.
whispered words of affection
broken into lies once more
past possible escapes haunting
those blades could've dug deeper
the fall could've looked shorter
headlights could've approached quicker
but the end slipped by me
expression of inner emotion
thwarted by the constant unkindness
can this devastated world
close its eyes and forget
the legacy i'd leave behind

could spread certain despair
but i don't think twice
they need a glimpse into this pain

The Deadliest of Poisons

Written: 2004

A feeling so strong Burns inside Blackened Hearts
Ripping, Tearing, Clawing away at my Soul
Tears of wretched Despair fall at random moments
They eat my Flesh away when they land on this Infected skin
Endlessly the Ashes of my Charred Heart fall away
They're carried through my Poisoned Blood
My Strength is fading Away now
My Soul will soon be utter Nothingness
Will I ever Feel again? Will Love ever come back again?
Love...the Deadliest of Poisons
Devouring every healthy being on this Cold Earth
Infecting them with False Belief
A Belief that someone they Care for will learn to See them
How Deceiving this Intoxication will always be
For it will Always End in Bleeding Hearts
An push the Memory of Happiness away Forever...

My Own Ending

Written: 2006

When the rain falls from above
Catch it
Hold it in your hand
Keep it only for yourself
This is what you must do
...I am told
Deserving of special treatment?
How can this be?
I don't. I'm worthless.
Infecting, nothing but acidic
Poisoning all those
Who dare to reach closeness
Constantly hurting them
Forever deceiving them
My presence doesn't belong
Not in this sacred land
My time on earth is short
But I can't wait for the end
I'll write my own ending

Darkness

Written: (2004-2006?)

As I live alone in this world
Darkness
My only companion
Darkness
I've grown to love one thing
Darkness
Blind and desperate
I find myself each day
Searching
For new "friends"
You see, a "friend" will
Betray you
Disobey you
Slay you
My friend
Darkness
Listens to me
Consoles me
Accepts me
I've grown to love one person
Darkness

As I stand lost
Before me lies
The path of lies
Taking me places
I'd wish to never see
But I'll keep
Darkness
By my side
Traveling blindly together
Darkness
Guides me
Forever stays
I've grown to love one power
Darkness
Leads me
Steers me
Will never leave me behind
Avoiding complications
Obstacles that threaten
To disrupt the
Darkness
Great protector
I've grown to love one thing
Darkness
My only friend

Again and Again and Again

Written: 2005

Scarred by your viciousness
Filled with screaming rage
Lost in the love that killed me
Torn apart with jealousy
Dreaming of cold death
Crazed because of care
Drifting away slowly...
Slit my wrists
Watch the blood flow
The deepest red
Spills to the floor
Stitch myself again
You rip me open again
Again and again and again

Sleep with the Knife

Written: 2005

It's harder now than ever before
I live and breathe, unfortunate
This deadly life has smothered me
Into the darkness I once confided in
One thought always creeps into my crowded mind
One thing I cannot bring myself NOT to focus on
One thing that continues to torture me
But I am comforted...why??
Why is the mere thought that you might love me
(Love me in the way I have always loved you)
Why so consoling, and still so fatal?
Why are you the one in my infected dreamland?
Questions with no answers...
It seems the foundation of my life is built on such
But it's over now as I have grown tired of waiting
Through forever with deadly crushes, poisonous love
Disease of love, spreading like anthrax
Through my increasingly defenseless body
I weep at night and lie by day
It's written in the starry night sky

That I shall never have that "happily ever after"
And so, I kiss my knife goodnight.

91

Letting the Blade Slide

Written: 2005

As the blade slides
Across my burning flesh
Allowing release
Of my bloody poison within
I recall the memories of those
Who hurt me the most
Those who said they cared
I wince, not from the pain...
But from their betrayal
They abandoned me
Stranded me alone
With just this blade
They gave it to me
Time has gone by
Passed the moment to ignore
It must be used. Now.
I'll hold it dear to my heart
Never will it leave me
Like so many others have
And I won't stop cutting

Until I have every mark
One for each of you who hurt me

When a Heart Fades

Written: 2004

My tears pour out a bloody mess,
As my heart continues to fall away
Crushed, my wounded soul within screams
An open, gaping gash is my entire life
Happiness forgotten, smiles extinguished
I lost love again.
My brokenness is not felt by any other
Struggling, fighting for my breath
Past memories racing fly by my eyes
They become all that I see, they become me
Present predicaments slaughter them dead
Dead, a welcoming word in time all around
Should I keep feeling this way forever?
Perhaps death shall end my pain and sorrow
It can be quick, this trigger so accepting
One rapid pull, and it's all over soon...
Then they are all standing 'round
Dressed in black, chanting some prayer
I only hope that they find what it's like
When tears fall as blood
A broken heart continues to fade

Part Three:
Refocus

Tears in the Moonlight

Written: September 27, 2009

Dance for the moon in solemn respect
Stare up at the face that gazes on you
A beautiful portrait it paints each night

The stars flicker, winking down upon
All the world sleeps sound in the black
But not I, awake, staring blankly above

No one can see in the depth of the night
What happens to me, I'm cold and alone
These walls imprison, I'm trapped here

No one can see in the depth of the night
In the glow of the eve with only myself
Only then will they fall, my tears in the moonlight

When only to know broken heartedness
Where else does a wounded soul turn?
But to the night and all its forgiveness

I shall guard myself that much more
As I decide, once again, to begin anew
This time remembering what has been told true

Who I Am Without Him

Written: October 12, 2009

No, not what I expected
But I moved on and left it
Alone in the darkness
Where I used to be

Believe it or not
I found myself surrounded
By the love of those
Who truly matter now

While they won't place blame
They can't see my heart
Don't know what it was
Before the beautiful change

I'd heard expression of old
"All's fair in love and war"
But for me, love WAS war
And I finally won

It was no simple surrender,
Though it may so appear
I just decided to find
Who I am without him

Slumber Soundly

Written: October 14, 2009

Sleeping soundly, Heaving sighs
Forgotten woes dream no more do I
Nightly solemn, I know believe new
Content in love's absence, No longer blue
Thoughts past of then so used me
Nearer to mine heart I do not wish see
May now the night fall e'er so soon
Embrace shall I, Slumber under true moon

Won. Too. Free. Door

Written: October 12, 2009

Tears.
Jeers.
Fear.
Here.

A battle.
A loss.

No. Not again. Never again.

No more recklessness
Bought a lock and key

I found something, I believed was new
It was there all along but I didn't know
Just looking inside myself, yes, it's true
I had the strength to get up and go

Me.
Mine.
Laugh.
Learn.

A choice.
A life.

Yes. Starting now. For the rest of my days.

No more recklessness
Bought a lock and key

I had to believe. I need to believe.
That this is my life and I can decide
Who I will love and the rules I'll abide
Sick of searching for my heart be retrieved

You.
Gone.
Good.
Bye.

A love, dismissed.
A care, released.

Now. Forever. Again. Always.

No more recklessness
Bought a lock and key

This fight is over, I finally won
Take the thoughts I think of you too
Just get out now and leave me free
Head this way, I'll show you the door

To My Patient, Loving Mother

Written: October 6, 2009

In my life, ever-changing and altered
There is one love I have known that never faltered

In the early hours of that late August morn
It was into her life that I was then born

And she held me tight in a soft warm wrap
As I made tiny baby noises there in her lap

Her daughter was there, her mother too
Soundless, all gazing at this life mine anew

Once all was arranged she would take me home
Unaware that she would be soon alone

As I ponder now what she must have felt
When the cards she drew were poorly dealt

Sadness consumes me, for I miss her so
When trial arose, it was to her I would go

But as I am stuck so far way away

It is here in this state I shall now stay

A woman of bravery, as best described
Put me in her shoes and I doubt I'd survive
She held it together, for she knew that she must
And I thank her now for all she did for us

There were moments I recall she worked extra hard
And all she asked of me was to take care of the yard

I paid her no mind, placed her requests on a shelf
Her selfish little boy thought but of only himself

Try as she might, it was quite impossible to succeed
In teaching me then to respect her maternal creed

Yet she did well with me, though she speaks otherwise
It was to her I confided my laughter and cries

And though at my summer camp her baton she twirled
I never truly regretted being born into her world

I value our relationship and cherish our smiles
My love for her spans immeasurable miles

So to my patient, loving mother I proudly say
I thank God that you're mine, each and every day

~Dedicated to Mom~

Sofia

Written: November 12, 2008

Serenity swims in her warm brown eyes
Open and honest, she deserves your trust
Forever believing in herself, in you, and in your dreams
Inescapable kindness topped with a melodic laughter
Always there, no matter how far

Revel in her tender joy, she'll make you smile
Angelic and gentle... she's always encouraging
May she grace you with her presence, whoever you are
In her smile, you'll find no falsehood
Reach out for a friendship with her
Everlasting patience makes her an exceptional best friend
Zis is ze end of ze poem

~Dedicated to Sofia M. Ramirez~

Kristi

Written: September 10, 2009

Kindness is alight within her eyes
Respect her, she deserves it
In tough spots, her temper won't rise
Smiles always upon her beautiful face
Try not to upset her though,
It's futile; she'll win any case

Dear to my heart, she'll always be
On a road to finding herself
Yet to me she's already found
Life-long trust and love in me
Ever mine, ever yours, we shall stay

~Dedicated to Kristi M. Doyle~

*When I Told You
(We Were Friends Forever)*

Written: May 5, 2009

Do you remember summer days with me?
Can you recall living perfectly, calmly carefree?
All those days together were always a joy for me
We may not've always seen eye-to-eye
But with our heads put together
Our dreams often reached the sky

When I remember you...
...and I frequently do
I remember the laughter, I remember the love
When I journey back to that image of us
I remember back when there was no fear
Nothing but laughter, nothing but love

We held onto the secrets said under sworn solemn oath
Hidden away, they'd never be known
And I never liked that time apart
When I picked up the phone, it was you on the other end

I always wanted you right by my side

But I never noticed it was because you were my only best friend

When I remember you...
...and I frequently do
I remember the laughter, I remember the love
When I journey back to that image of us
I remember back when there was no fear
Nothing but laughter, nothing but love

We were absolute opposites
But shared the same beating heart
If I knew then, what I know now...
For now I'll just remember your face
And how it looked when I told you
That we were friends forever

~Dedicated to "Feuer Frei"~

29

Written: October 14, 2009

I remember when the clock struck two
And for 29 minutes I'm taken back to you
As memories race, like 29 horses, by
Stampede across my thoughts, I heave a sigh
It wasn't 'til now that I came to terms
The life I failed to live...I've confirmed
On that fateful 29th day of a November long ago
I swore my heart to you because of love's glow
It was real; love as now I loved so then
And I can journey back to when I held your hand
You, by my side always, needn't look too far
My best friend I held tight, my lucky star
Every 29th day was a joyous event
Thoughts turn now, to that of lament
Because I mangled the love unintentionally
Stupidly selfish, I thought of only me
It was never my plan to make you despise
But as I reached for the truth, I found 29 lies
Years have passed, but I still think of us
How I wish it had worked, without this fuss

So every 29th day, as I age another year

Know that I think of you, and wish you were near

~Dedicated to Lisa M. Stowers~

Fields

Written: 2004

Scarcely believing in feelings so true
Guides unhappiness to incomprehensive sorrow

So be steadfast in what you believe
And let not your heart be troubled

For when you believe in that which is true
Your heart will guide you to great golden fields

Roll in these fields of happiness and friendship
And you will know that life is wonderful

Only Want to Help

Written: 2004

Words cannot begin to describe
The pain I feel for her.
How can she let that happen?
If only she could take it back…
Being the only one that knows
Makes me feel trusted.
But deep down inside
I can't help but cringe.
Now she thinks I've judged her,
But I could never do that
I'm her friend forever.
I just try to help.

Skin (Live Good)

Written: February 12 and October 22, 2009

If you're worried about them
And what they might say
Don't give in to their scorn
You need simply be you
This is your life
You've been given a chance
Let your light shine
Live and breathe exhilarated
Immerse yourself within what you love
Do whatever it takes to succeed
Cherish each day's moments
Because they shall soon be memories
And remember to be cautious
For you could blink
And all the world may shift
Listen to this advice my friend
Walk with your head held high
Believe in yourself
And you, oh, trust me
Will find out who you are
Just live good in your own skin

Temperamental Vanity

Written: October 18, 2009

There are times when I walk in shame
Feeling as if the world mocks my pain
But somehow now, I've noticed a change
Something happening in my head, heart and soul
After all I've endured through this, my life
I don't care if its wrong, being in love with me
So smugly enjoying this temperamental vanity
I am who I am and I stand tall all alone
I did the work to find what I needed
To construct who I am, make me myself
It's what I do, what I say, what I wear
But more what I've learned, and how I've grown
I've finally become me, flying solo so long
Reached inside, found the right nerve ends
Gave them a tug towards a happier trail
And so thankful I found the undiscovered me
Now when I see my reflection I hold my head high
Because I'm an artist and I love what I do
I have family and friends that support and care
And I've got plenty of laughter and love to share

Be Free

Written: September 29, 2008

Run.
Faster. Harder.
Breaking through the branches
Golden sun blazing down
Whipping through the air
Exhilaration raging through
Inching closer to flight
Heart lifting higher
You're breaking free now
Sprinting into mountain air
Passion swelling within your heart
Creating the unstoppable
Wings of freedom
Finally unleashed

Spider's Web

Written: September 26, 2008

Staring intently, serenely and still
You fiercely form your intricate design
Everything you are and need
Contained in one invisible entity
Your home and shelter, beauty unbound
How delicately to be created
Now divine in the perfect place
Branches around shares dances with the wind
As the setting sun paints the sky tranquil
That single tear falls from my eye
Strong and armed you feel you are
Defended within your fort abstraction
Unaware of horrific dangers ever so near
This silken home you have made
Easily destroyed, menacing creature
But my heart bleeds for you
This protection you seek is a nature
I cannot bring myself to pull away
And I won't leave with nothing
As have I so many memories before

Rest well my arachnid of friend
For I shall never, ever harm you

118

No Offense

Written: October 23, 2008

Spark. A thought's ignited
As I'm unable to keep it in
No matter how harming it could be
It's out of my dumb mouth
Before I have a chance to stop it

I admit, it's my fault
My mouth is as big as can be
And once again, I've done it again
Someone is hurt, and it's because of me
But I find it too hard to reel it in

Don't take offense to what I say
Ignorance. Awkardness. Idiocracy.
I'm caught up inside of me
But keep on livin'. Keep on believin'.
Simply maintain your jubilation

Who knows the damages I have caused
My wires have come loose inside
And I don't hold the right to ask you why

Why are you angry? Why are you crying?
What is the matter with you?

But you came to me, confronted me
And it was you, yes you, who made me see
The damaging words that I've inflicted
Hearts were wounded and yet to be mended
And it was this you said to me:

Don't be offensive with what you say
Discipline. Intelligence. Think before you speak
And practice some self-control
Just think it through, and trust me
You just might change the nation.

~Dedicated to Emily R. Lucas~

This Trek Be Made

Written: September 29, 2009

I want, with all my heart, to make it to those distant hills
Fight my way through the obstacles that lie in waiting
If only I had the strength, the dedication, the focus
Those mountains of triumph have always called to me
Even many years ago, as a boy, carefree in my youth,
I knew deep down inside, that they held a great purpose
And every warm summer day, every cool autumn night since
I gaze upon them in serene, solemn respect...awestruck
Thinking to myself how envious I am of they who made it
Those who fought the briar, made the journey, reaped the reward
Motivation should arise, yet I am left melancholy
And, I often wonder, must this trek be made now?
If I wait too long, will there be anything left for me?

Starlight 12.2

Written: October 4, 2009

Dear Starlight,
I wonder to myself what brought me here...
Could it have been intricate accidents?
Perhaps a greater plan has pre-destined me
Moving the wandering heart to a far-off land
As an escape artist, time won't find me
I distance myself from the world I once knew
"Have you found yourself yet?" You ask.
I believe in certain truths universal
Laughter and Light, Brilliance and Brotherhood
Honesty and Affection, Faith and Inspiration
"When the moment is right,
Will you find what you're looking for?"
I'll leave you tonight without an answer
As I have been left so many times before
Alone on a sandy shore, my mind races still
Your light shines bright in the dead of 20 past
It's a beautiful white that holds still no resolve
Lost in thought, far from those I love...
Shall I ever find myself home again?

Mental more, a mystery still, I suddenly realize:
I haven't yet found where my home is.

Reset Life (Start Again)

Written: September 9, 2009

Reset the time on my life
Give me the option to redo my rights
Give me the chance to undo my wrongs

Reset the time on my life
I need to find a way to set this straight
I need to find a way to not be too late

Reset the time on my life
What can I do with the hours given?
What can I say with the minutes left?

Reset the time on my life
I never even had a first chance
I never realized it at first glance

Reset the time on my life
Can't I just restart from those early days?
Can't I just relive and make some changes?

Reset the time on my life
All I need to change happened way back when
All I need is the chance to start again

War

Written: 2004

Separated into many parts
I can't decide
Who am I?
What should I do?
When I'm this
They're mad
When I'm that
The others are mad
I'm torn
My life is split
Who can tell me
What's going on?
Who should I be?
Why should I?
What if I lose someone
So important to me?
Would I survive?
This war being fought
Deep down inside,
Pulls at my heart,
My brain, my soul…

I'll have to choose
Which life to live
The other will die,
Buried in the past.
They'll have to forgive,
Forget, and worry no more
I have to decide
Who wins this war.

SocioPsycho

Written: September 28, 2009

I took care in the words I so patiently wrote
Spent years becoming who I am today
I survived humiliation and endured oppression
I did it myself, yes, all on my own
Now after all these years, these many words
The side of me, patiently waiting to be known
That part of me aching to be newly seen
Has been mocked and ignored all the more
So now before me, a choice lies in waiting
The toughest decision I've yet to face
The time has come for a transformation
I have my options, I have pros and cons
Perhaps I choose freedom from social opinion
A choice leaving me unaffected
From thoughts and feelings of others
A chance to think of only myself
Another opportunity is before me in plain sight
An option leaving me crazed and carefree
Escaping the real, driven to be wild
I'll get what I want, and when I want it
Two clear chances for freedom

But which shall I choose when the time comes?
The path of selfishness? Or the path of wildness?
As the crossroads become ever-close
The names of them become ever-clear
Socio…Psycho... Which Path is right for me?

Experience the Light

Written: 2005; Rewritten: Fall 2008

Stranded here, alone. Again.
My desolate Dreamland raging
Throughout all of my body.
Slowing eating away my summer sunshine.
Extinguished fire light.
Ruptured, broken happiness
Screaming, crying, leave it behind
Run...faster and faster
Through a forest of dreams
Dark, empty dreams...Lost.
I, blind, scream out heartache
As my flesh, cut open again
Drips blood black as coal
My mind has been terrorized
Surrounding darkness presses down
I find myself suffocating slowly
An infection spreading through
I shall soon cease to be...
But I can only pray it will be swift
Unable to withstand outstanding heartache
If only to find a way to break free

Find the path...the path of Hope
Can it be You? Are You calling for me?
I long for the rescue you might offer.
Help me. Save me. Find me here.
Pull me into the sunshine again
The light...I had never imagined...
Knowing only bleak, bitter darkness
But to experience the light uncharted...
But can my dead heart be restored?
These many questions I have...
...Do you have the answers?
I crave freedom from anguish
Look to the sky...are You the answer?

Set Me Free

Written: 2004

Locked beneath this outer being
A soul within tries to escape
Fighting and struggling
It seeks to find a way out
No exit can be found here
This soul slows down
It begins to realize
That this is the end
The end of its long life
For the one on the outside
Has chosen something new
Time flies by day and night
Fading away, it's almost gone
But something has changed
It appears something's been brought back
The spirit is hence reborn anew
Growing stronger and stronger
Now again is in control
A soul's prayer was answered,
"Set me free..."

Don't Give Up

Written: 2004

I fear the worst has come about
Who can tell what they feel inside?
Far worse is the distress uncontrolled within,
By no one human may these things disperse.
For the world has hate, not compassion.
Not that anyone wouldn't want to forgive,
Since all is contained beyond comprehension
Why won't someone answer these bewilderments?
Will there soon be that truth?
Make known that which is unknown?
Don't lose hope, we'll soon know
Even if it's not on this earthly soil.
Answers are found later down this road.
Don't give up...

Fear Not

Written: September 4, 2009

Fear is like a wall
You hide behind
But it is built
On a shaky foundation

Fear is like a window
You stay behind
But the panes will blur
The world around you

Fear can become a shelter
But it will never protect

Fear can become a promise
But one that is never kept

Fear will always be there
But it won't keep you company

Fear will always follow you
But it can't always catch you

Not if YOU stay away
Not if you forever pray

Pray that life will remain
Forever in the control of your creator

Your Wall built on sturdy ground
Your Window showing the wonders around
Your Shelter to always keep you warm
Your Promise,
Your Companion,
Your Father,
Your Friend,
Forever.

Yes Yes Soundmachine (Music Love)

Written: October 9, 2009

The harmony, the melody,
The chords, the words,
The way I'm fueled to jive
I say, "Yes! Yes!" To the soundmachine

As my jig continues
The happiness swells
Different than what I know
I say, "Yes! Yes!" To the soundmachine

It's the music love
I can't remain still
My body can't resist a move
I say, "Yes! Yes!" To the soundmachine

A perfect ensemble
I've found a true love
Uplifted. Overwhelmed. Happy.
I say, "Yes! Yes!" To the soundmachine

It Began With a Sneeze

Written: September 23, 2009

Itching...twitching...agitated
Can't see clearly, eyes so hazy
Certain burning deep within
Eventually all will come out
Complete release will leave me free
From all the discomfort built up inside
That fortress shall come crashing down
As all is swept away at just the right moment
Forceful and violent, it begins a new day
I'll know I'm alive and that I'm OK.

Never Wake Me

Written: 2004

I can't take this anymore
I feel myself stiffening
I tried so hard to avoid this
But it won't stop…
Never.
Its constant torture drives me to insanity
A crazed child can destroy anything…
I hope it knows...for its own sake
That it will never torture me again
Never.
My teeth bared,
My rage surging,
My fist clenched,
I raise it high and bring it down…
Never,
Will that alarm wake me again.

I Haven't Met Me

Written: October 4, 2009

They see me... but is it the real me?
I see nothing. Where is my reflection?

It's because I haven't met me yet

I haven't experienced the commitment
My knowledge on the subject is vague

It's because I haven't met me yet

When I dream of what could be
And wonder why I don't get what I desire

It's because I haven't met me yet

Those in my life who hold dear to their heart
That which I have yet in to take part

It's because I haven't met me yet

All this time I've spent in doubt and shadowed envy
Carries me to inward thought and selfishness

It's because I haven't met me yet

Maybe I'm close to the end of the wait
Perhaps there will come a day when I win the prize

I still haven't met me yet

I await a day when I live in newfound maturity
When I can look at myself and say, "It's nice to know you."

Because I haven't met me yet

My Utmost Gratitude and Appreciation
(In Other Words… Thanks)

My utmost gratitude and appreciation are reserved for anyone and everyone that has ever encouraged me to pursue my goals as a writer, as well as all those who supported me, whether financially, emotionally, or otherwise. My thanks go out to Mom, for giving me life, for teaching me how to love, and for being my Mom, the only one I could ever want. Without your influence, I wouldn't be the man I am today. Ralph, for entering my mother's life and mine, and being the father I never had. I'm thankful for the decisions you made that helped shape my life. Amanda, for taking me in, for teaching me how to live, and for being the best older sister I could have ever wanted. Nate, for welcoming me into your life, for loving Amanda, and for teaching me to be a man. Dad, for passing your creative gene to me. I'm sure you're who I got it from. Sof & Kristi, for every little thing you do for me that shows me you love me. You're my best friends and I can't imagine life without you both. Daniel, for everything you've ever said or done to encourage my writing career. Laura, for bringing a smile to my face when I need it most. Jill & Lindsey, for being the friends I never have to fear losing, I love you forever, nothing will change that. Hannah, for being a loyal friend and fan, even when times were rough (Also, for senior year). Lauren, for inspiring, encouraging, guiding and critiquing my writing, you're my mentor. If it wasn't for you, I might not have continued writing. Lisa, for being forgiving in every possible way. Chelsie & Anna, for standing up for me, when I couldn't do it myself. Suzy, for being there for me when it really counts. Joyce, for keeping everything real; I need the reality check from time to time. Leah, for helping me find humor in all aspects of life. Liz & CJ, for growing accustomed to my ways and eventual writer lifestyle, you guys are great roommates. Chris H., for being a great best friend when we were. Col, for every memory that made the year in the Bay amazing, I'll never forget any of them. You're the closest thing to a brother I've ever known. Laurie, Dan & Jennifer, for being the greatest "back-up" family I've ever had. Kyle, Kirstyn & the Palguts, for loving me and my family, the way we love you. Trisha, for believing in me against all odds, and for being someone I never felt reluctant confiding in. Grandma & Grandpa, for always being proud of your only grandson. Sandra, for the laughter we were once able to share. My whole family, for loving me. My teachers throughout my life that helped shape me and my writing for the better, most notably, Mrs. Cathy Harryman and Professor Carmen Jay. Also, Mrs. Jennifer Van Wyk, Mr. Eric Semler, Mrs. Hope Frey, Mrs. Laura Wilson-Liebmann, Mrs. Suzanne Heinz, Professor Linda Lee, and Professor Rosemarie Adams. My thanks are also extended to the wonderful Colbie Caillat and Taylor Swift, for being my heroes. Other musicians I'd like to thank are Miley Cyrus, Joanna Pacitti, Kate Voegele, Lesley Roy, Shiny Toy Guns and Breaking Benjamin. Without the words you have written, I would have had difficulty writing myself. You *all* inspire me. Lastly, I'd like to thank Metro Community Church and BigStuf Camp in Panama City Beach, Florida for making it impossible for me to fall away from my faith in God, who I also want to thank…for my life, my heart, my mind, and for finally showing me that I have a talent.

Author Bio

Stuart James was born August 29, 1988 in Richmond, Virginia. He was raised in the small town of Collinsville, Illinois until he graduated high school. After high school, he relocated to San Diego, California. He currently lives in San Diego and is studying Education, with a minor in English. He hopes to return to the Midwest at some point to teach middle school, while continuing to write.